Blockchain Explained:

A Technology Guide to the Bitcoin and Cryptocurrency Fintech Revolution

By: R.J. Simmons

Published by:

R.J. Simmons and Random Technologies

4409 HOFFNER AVENUE, SUITE 347

Belle Isle, FL 32812

www.SparrowPublications.com

Table of Contents

Disclaimer 1

A Warning. 3

Introduction 5

The Basics 9
    What Does It All Mean?... 12
    What A Blockchain Really Is And Why It Matters...... 14
    They Are Manipulating Your Data! 15
    Isn't It MY Money? 16
    How The Internet Joined The Blockchain.................. 18
    Greedy Banks – Including Hackers And Price Fixers.... 20

What Is Bitcoin?... 23
    Smart Money?... 26
    The Value Of A Coin?... 27
    What About International Trade?............................... 29

How To Invest Safely In Bitcoin....................................... 31
    Other Ways To Invest 33
    Adding Bitcoin To Your Business 34
    What Is Ethereum? 36

Conclusion 39

Additional Resources 43

Disclaimer

The author has made every attempt to be as accurate and complete as possible in the creation of this publication/PDF, however he / she **does not warrant or represent at any time that the contents within are accurate due to the rapidly changing nature of the Internet.** The author assumes no responsibility for errors, omissions, or contrary interpretation of the subject matter herein. Any perceived slights of specific persons, peoples, or organizations other published materials are unintentional and used solely for educational purposes only.

This information is not intended for use as a source of legal, business, accounting or financial advice. All readers are advised **to seek services of competent professionals in the legal, business, accounting, and finance field.** No representation is made or implied that the reader will do as well from using the suggested techniques, strategies, methods, systems, or ideas; rather it is presented for news value only.

The author does not assume any responsibility or liability **whatsoever** for what you choose to do with this information. Use your own judgment. Consult appropriate professionals before starting a business or making ANY investment. Any perceived remark, comment or use of organizations, people mentioned and any resemblance to characters living, dead or otherwise, real or fictitious does not mean that they support this content in any way but is provided for news value / information only.

There are no guarantees of income made, and understand investment is often very risky, especially cryptocurrencies. NO PROMISES ARE MADE of any kind and all information provided is for information value only!

Readers are cautioned to reply on their own judgment about their individual circumstances to act accordingly. By reading any document, the reader agrees that under no circumstances is the author responsible for any losses, direct or indirect, that are incurred as a result of use of the information contained within this document, including - but not limited to errors, omissions, or inaccuracies.

A Warning. . .

Buying, selling and trading **cryptocurrencies** is inherently risky, especially if you base any reliance on this as a means to making money.

This guide is for basic information only and you must do your own research, investigation and proof of what I say in this guide is viable for you and your unique situation.

While many **cryptocurrency** trades happen daily, and the vast majority of trades are satisfactory as an investment and safety vehicle, moneymaking is not typically the reason.

This guide was written with the express purpose of giving you the information you need to make intelligent decisions as to whether or not you wish to consider crypto currencies is a superior and safer method to current financial institutions, such as large banks.

Most people invest in cryptocurrencies **as a security and privacy factor**. While you can and eventually should be able to make additional money, this is by no means guarantee in any way.

Please use this information wisely. Check with professionals in investments and seek financial consultation as I cannot guarantee anything that you choose to do, as I have no way of supervising how you use this information.

Introduction

Many people have now heard of cryptocurrencies like **Bitcoin**. You may even wonder what is so special about it all. Is the technology behind Bitcoin really as powerful as people are suggesting? Is Bitcoin **a serious investment** given the volatility of prices for the currency and current market instabilities? Why should you consider investing in Bitcoin?

Now enter another term - "blockchain".

This foundational, revolutionary and highly promising tool / construct supports as well as expands **whole new industries** to emerge based on its merits; just like what HTML was to the foundation of the Internet.

HTML evolved to meet the demand of peer to peer exchanges by creating a massive "blockchain" called the **World Wide Web**.

The blockchain is now one of the best tools / constructs we use to protect ourselves in an often less than honest society that requires more and more of our privacy and personal information. All in the name of doing business with major institutions, like banks, who scrutinize everything we do with *our* money because the banks consider it *their* money (even though it is YOUR account and currency).

The blockchain prevents the need to expose our every decision about our money and personal choices, while attempting to regain our own trust, instead of relying on institutions that can and do sell our privacy and trust to the highest bidder, while charging exorbitant fees for everything we do based on those decisions:

"A blockchain is a public ledger of all Bitcoin transactions that have ever been executed. It is constantly growing as 'completed' blocks are added to it with a new set of recordings. The blocks are added to the blockchain in a linear, chronological order. Each node (computer connected to the Bitcoin network using a client that performs the task of validating and relaying transactions) gets a copy of the blockchain, which gets downloaded automatically upon joining the Bitcoin network. The blockchain has complete information about the addresses and their balances right from the genesis block to the most recently completed block."

Source: http://www.investopedia.com/terms/b/blockchain.asp

Yet this is just the beginning of what a blockchain really is.

From the sake of a potential investor, the blockchain offers **unparalleled safety and security**; unlike almost all forms of transactions that involve the exchange of personal information to third parties, as well as access to your money without ongoing consent for each transaction.

A blockchain is a form of **a technical construct** that is created and sustained via peer to peer relationships (computer to computer).

The blockchain is designed to provide absolute and irrefutable proof of any and all transactions. Now single users can safely participate in trade and transactions without fear of governmental agencies, industries and watchdog / information brokers from collecting data on you personally and using this information to cause issues or even harm you personally. It is the new trust factor.

Decentralization is critical to how it all works, and shows just how beneficial this information can be for you and your financial future, including protecting your privacy.

In addition, exploring cryptocurrencies adds an entirely new dimension and possibilities for safety and security.

Some people master cryptocurrencies to the point where they actually earn money on most of the transactions. That is entirely possible as well.

There are exciting new ways to share cryptocurrency technologies that can actually help your business to grow too.

This eBook is here to explore all these things with you.

Finally you hold in your hands the real power of understanding exactly what Bitcoin, blockchains and crypto currencies all can mean to you.

The three concepts come together to offer you real safety and security for true investments that you will be able to count on, even if the very financial institutions are collapsing all around you.

That is some real power, wouldn't you agree? Let's explore this fascinating topic.

The Basics

You just might be asking yourself what is all the excitement over digital currency? What is the big deal and what are the benefits of using electronic money?

Digital currency has actually been around for years and any time you make a purchase online, you are actually using a form of digital currency; but it is backed by a bank and "digital dollars" so most of us conclude this transaction is not a digital currency exchange. Yet it is . . .

Many of us use credit cards every day and never give it a second thought. Yet every time you swipe your card to make a trade (purchase) you are doing several not so good things:

- ✓ You give away the right to your privacy as third parties sell your information (purchase habits, income, what you buy, how much money you have, etc.).

- ✓ You engage the services of a third party middleman who charges you fees.

- ✓ You give away your private banking / CC information to potential hackers. (Banks are one of their biggest targets).

- ✓ You create a transaction that can be changed, altered or used in a fraudulent attempt to take money from you.

All of these things happen each and every day when you use a traditional financial institution to process any and all transactions that occur on a daily basis from your account.

Yet true digital or crypto currency transactions, have many advantages over traditional financial institutions:

✓ **Cheaper / NO Transaction Fees** – Almost all transaction fees are from credit cards, banks and third party processors.

✓ **Works Well Online** – Online merchants are beginning to embrace the new currencies like Bitcoin by the tens of thousands. There are many reasons for this, as we will discuss.

✓ **NO International Fees** – This is huge as many countries move to add huge fees when it comes to moving monies from country to country.

✓ **Big Banks HATE It** – We all know that the biggest banks are all involved in politics, money manipulation and other nefarious activities that the typical person does not like to support. The biggest banks have all come out against cryptocurrencies, which is a great reason to be supportive of it.

✓ **NO Account Fees / Overdraft Fees etc**. – considering banks each year take millions of dollars just in overdraft fees from people that have no money, and charge fees for almost everything, this is a great advantage and way to opt out from banks.

✓ **Easy Account Approval** – if you ever bounced a check you could have problems opening an account. Creating most cryptocurrency accounts is easy, fast and often free with no credit check.

✓ **Restore Complete Control** – now you can have complete control over every transaction you do with digital currency. You don't need approval; you do not need a government official or bank employee to approve any transaction even for overseas transfers.

✓ **Better Protection Than ANY Bank** – As you will see later in this eBook, banks are actually very risky places to keep your money.

✓ **Protection Against Theft** – Cryptocurrencies like Bitcoin cannot be physically stolen from you, or taken from you without your direct approval. Money in a bank can be seized, frozen, delayed or taken from you at any time! This has happened to millions of people. Digital currencies are encrypted and only YOU can authorize their transfer, no one else.

✓ **Banks Involved In Criminal Activity** – Many big banks today have been caught laundering drug money, giving money to terrorists, taking people's property even if they paid in full for it, loan fraud, investor fraud . . . the list goes on.

What Does It All Mean?

Large financial institutions, like big banks, are at the heart many of the problems in our society. Part of this is the illusion that many banks are just too big to fail.

We've seen in our lifetime literally **dozens of high price banker bailouts** to people who consistently violate the laws that they are supposed to follow.

Over the many years, banking systems and financial conditions have all organized as to work against the typical person who thinks they need their services.

Perhaps this is part of the reason why new currencies like Bitcoin are becoming so incredibly popular.

People are tired of the boom or bust cycle of banks and having to bail out financial institutions that cannot seem to balance their own budgets but expect the average person to do so and have to pay to make up the difference.

Banks are under an obligation not to create any amount of money yet they demand money from their users, the public and of course the taxpayer, to the tune of billions.

The new wave of bankers are much more concerned with government contracts, and loaning money to large businesses in such a way that the taxpayer gets stuck with most of the bill.

Because of this, we are giving most commercial banks **far more control over our money and finances than they should have.**

For example, during the 2008 financial crisis, because banks were loaning money to just about anyone (the housing bubble and stock market crash, remember that?), and few people could actually pay back these loans, it caused a huge collapse and banks ran out of money.

Governments had to involve themselves to "fix" the problem and give hundreds of millions of dollars to these institutions so they would have sufficient money to keep operating.

Even though governments gave vast amount of monies to these failing banks, banks still took money out of people's accounts without giving people the option to do so. **For example, in Cyprus, many account holders lost some or even most of their money as it was taken directly out of their accounts without approval to "pay" for the bank's mistakes.**

All of this boils down to WHY cryptocurrencies are becoming so popular. The emerging technology (the blockchain) makes this all possible; finally a way to EXCLUDE big banks from totally running our finances, controlling our money and preventing us access when we most need it.

NO MORE! It is time to explore cryptocurrencies, what they really can do for you, and the technology, the blockchain and how it all works to finally protect YOUR future and YOUR money from would be bankster crooks.

What A Blockchain Really Is And Why It Matters

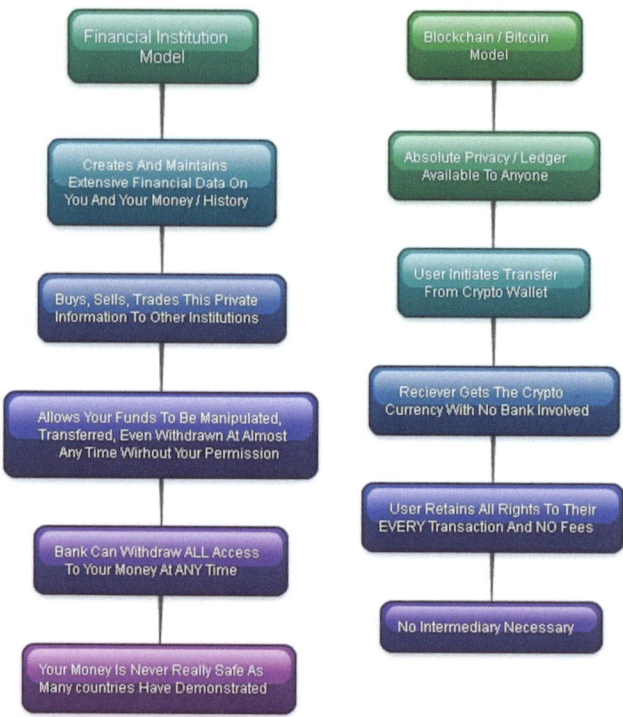

The blockchain is the foundational and most basic **linear expression** that is at the heart of utilizing cryptocurrency technology.

It records all transactions in a very powerful and sequential way **that prevents the erasure** of such informational blocks that are all linked together. The blockchain offers real solutions to the many problems we face especially with retaining control over our money and privacy. Let's see how this all comes together.

They Are Manipulating Your Data!

Too many institutions **manipulate data** on a daily basis and can systematically change entire subroutines and databases, even whole algorithms to always make their institution and/or business benefit and you the consumer pay the price.

For example, if you went to a bank and made a deposit, the bank processes this request using their data, their rules and their policies. You have NO control over ANY of this.

This one act of "trust" is completely controlled by the banking institution, and YOU must fully rely on *their* record-keeping and any other types of applications to that singular transaction the bank deems important.

If your account was overdrawn, you could expect to pay expensive fees and not to have access to all of your money.

These institutions are in the business of **manipulating currencies** by creating fiat monies as well as using customer accounts to back it all, to the benefit of their stockholders and the detriment of the typical account holder.

The bank has complete autonomy and power to control that singular action and every action thereafter.

All that you can do is simply react to what the bank chooses to do with your money and try to mitigate negative circumstances to the best of your ability.

Isn't It MY Money?

When you join a bank, you create an account. You believe that this account is yours, but in reality the account is completely controlled, modified, altered or even changed on a daily basis contingent on bank policies, fees, current political events occurring in the nation, where the bank resides, and a variety of other events that act upon the account including other accounts and fraud issues.

For example, in Greece, banks collapsed and prevented people from having access to money in their account. Some of this was planned by the financial institutions that should have had **no authority** to be able to take money from customers for ANY reason, yet this is what happened.

Monies were taken right out of people's accounts that owed NOTHING to the bank and for no other reason than to help the bank survive its own mismanagement and fraud:

Source: http://www.libertynewsnow.com/greek-banks-to-steal-deposits-american-banks-next/article1740

The whole concept of a blockchain is to **decentralize** authority and power over your financial investments (and other private / trust exchanges) so that no bank or institution is ever capable of doing to you, what we have seen done in the nation of Greece, Spain, Germany, France, and recently here in the U.S., just to name a few.

Financial institutions not only systematically defraud their investors, but even **plan to do so** in the future at increments; especially when there is political upheaval, civil unrest or other forms manipulation including outright fraud from governments and other related institutions who join in this collusion.

This all boils down to an issue **of trust** and more and more people are discovering the importance of decentralizing many of the institutions they currently are interacting with.

Shouldn't you do the same?

Trust is everything:

"The blockchain cannot be described as just a revolution. It is a marching phenomenon, slowly advancing like a tsunami, and gradually enveloping everything along the way by the force of progression. Plainly, it is the second significant overlay on top of the Internet, just as the web was that first layer back in 1990. That new layer is mostly about trust, so we could call it the trust layer."

Source: https://www.amazon.com/Business-Blockchain-Practice-Application-Technology-ebook/dp/B01EIGP8HG

The issue of trust is now the central concern of all people. Without trust, you cannot have effective trade. This trade should happen without restrictions, without the necessity of third parties.

This is the real power of the blockchain. It allows people to come together in a way that will not be stopped. Finally you can have real peace of mind and it all happens around you. The blockchain cannot be stopped and will change the internet again and again.

How The Internet Joined The Blockchain

In the 80s, the Internet was barely understood until the **World Wide Web** overlay was launched. This was a practical design that utilized simplistic HTML as the newest way to communicate information; the first blockchain.

Due to the redundancy of the Internet and now the World Wide Web, millions and eventually billions of locations could now access data privately and almost immediately. This included online databases that could answer questions for people without the need for another human to be involved.

The information age had arrived. Once questions were answered, people began to crave more. The World Wide Web has shown that even a modest technology of peer-to-peer communications could be expanded upon to the point where we now have the current Internet, a massive series of databases all interconnected and overlapping each other.

Initially, the Internet was designed to allow **peer-to-peer** communications between colleges and eventually morphed into a way to prevent information and data from being completely restricted or even destroyed. If one system went down, redundant backups were ready and duplication became the real power of the Internet.

With the advent of all of this, **data security** soon became a challenge. So did anonymity of the end user. The dot com bubble showed the potential for abuse, with people investing in unrealistic business models simply due to the Top Level Domains that looked valuable.

Sure millions were made but much was also lost due to the over exposure of **confidential data** that could now be gathered by shadow programs that were now continuously mining the web.

Even the most inept investor, entrepreneur or opportunity seeker could clearly view the writing on the wall. People began to see that **trust** was and should be a new focus of blockchains. Guess what? They were right!

Greedy Banks – Including Hackers And Price Fixers

If everything you have read to this point hasn't been reason enough for you to get really excited about cryptocurrencies and using the Bitcoin blockchain, imagine being able to **permanently protect yourself from financial institutions** that are constantly being hacked, are involved in price-fixing and ultimately are required to report your activities so that the government can take its turn by taking more of your hard earned money (high taxes, fees, etc.).

Currently, the United States has **the highest tax bracket** for business in the entire world! Many other countries also follow suit, like France, where their taxation structure is so high, it discourages people from seeking full time employment.

Therefore, one of the best things that you can do to protect your money is **to invest in cryptocurrencies**.

Many large financial institutions have come out against cryptocurrencies because it removes them from the equation:

"The fact that Bitcoin is facing so much top-down antagonism from those particularly moneyed Western banks shows that **Bitcoin is on the right track. It won't be long before the average netizen realizes that Bitcoin is a better place to put ones savings than a bank account.** Bitcoin is ruffling the feathers of those that have been in monetary power for centuries, thus is the nature of paradigm shifts and change in general."

Source: https://www.cryptocoinsnews.com/banks-hate-bitcoin/

Large institutions are also susceptible **to hackers**. Banking systems are constantly under attack and even if these attacks are not discovered initially, they can still have grave consequences for millions of people and their accounts. In a rather informative report by **AmericanBanker. com** we see that most hacking is directed at financial institutions:

"This year's report is more weighted toward financial motivation than ever before," said Chris Novak, director of investigative response at Verizon Enterprise Solutions. "We've looked at different motivations — financial, espionage, and other categories like fun, ideology, or grudge. You've seen a lot of those other categories die down."

Below you can clearly see that ALL financial institutions are clearly at RISK, all the time from hackers. It is a constant problem that nobody should ignore. Your money is NOT safe:

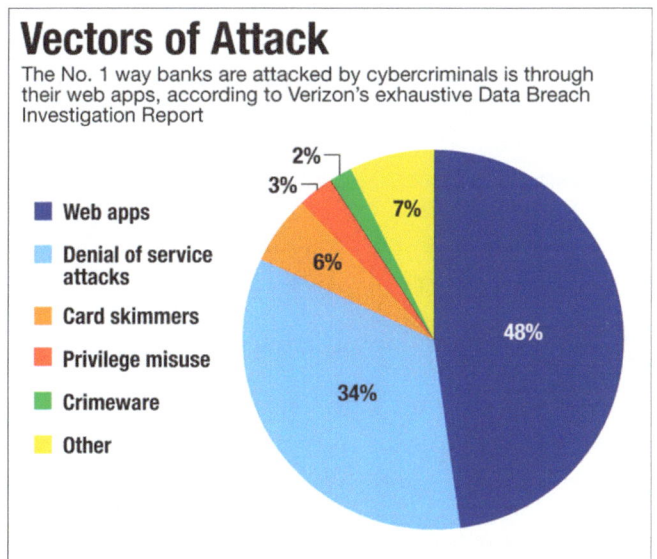

Sources: http://www.americanbanker.com/news/bank-technology/ where-banks-are-most-vulnerable-to-cyberattacks-now-1080671-1. html

In addition most banks are paying very low or even NEGATIVE interest.

This means that you will pay the bank for the privilege of keeping your money until such time that you must remove this money.

You can expect the following issues just to remove your money in the first place:

- ✓ **Earn little or no money** while the bank creates endless loans from your money.

- ✓ **The bank**, their database and everyone they deem ok now has access to your personal information.

- ✓ **The bank uses your account** and personal information to sell this to third parties.

- ✓ **The ability of the financial institutions to do almost anything** with your money while it is in their possession.

- ✓ **The government** can track everything that you do with your money thanks to the bank who hands over this information.

- ✓ **Money is made by the financial institution** from the sale of fiat currency based on your deposits.

- ✓ **Money you deposit** can be used to support many political or social projects you are opposed to.

Any one of these concerns is simply **unacceptable**.

If you are anything like me, I do NOT want financial institutions having and holding such power over me and my future. It is time to take the money away from them.

It may also be a moral obligation not to turn over your finances to people like this.

If you do, I promise you sooner or later, you will expose your savings to possible theft as well as excessive bureaucracy, fees, fines and over taxation.

What Is Bitcoin?

bit·coin
/ˈbitˌkoin/

noun

a type of digital currency in which encryption techniques are used to regulate the generation of units of currency and verify the transfer of funds, operating independently of a central bank.
"bitcoin has become a hot commodity among speculators"

- a unit of bitcoin.
  "bitcoins can be used for online transactions between individuals"

Cryptocurrencies are now being seriously looked at as one of the best potential investment strategies in an ever increasing dangerous and unstable world.

Banks worldwide are failing, entire governments are collapsing, and even though all of this is happening, cryptocurrencies are turning out to be one of the safest and potentially best harbors from the storms of uncertainty for your investments. Even the banks are now are trying to imitate Bitcoin Blockchain structures:

"Hackett claims the reason banks are now so interested in blockchain technology is they see it as a way to respond to the competitive threat that bitcoin poses to traditional money. While many financial institutions now claim to be interested in blockchain technology but not bitcoin, they ignore the fact that you need a cryptocurrency to make a blockchain. Hackett postulates that hyping the blockchain while denigrating bitcoin is an effort to blunt bitcoin's challenge to traditional currency."

Source: https://www.cryptocoinsnews.com/whats-behind-banks-hyping-blockchain-not-bitcoin-defensive-play-one-observer-claims/

Now that you see the power of cryptocurrencies, let's discuss Bitcoin, one of the very best types.

Bitcoin is a digital currency, plain and simple. It can be used to buy things electronically. The unique nature of Bitcoin allows people to exchange value directly from or to each other, without the necessity of involving any type of financial institution.

Because there are no governing financial institutions, no one directly controls the currency. There is a limited amount of coins in circulation, and nobody creates or mints them but rather they are a measured and assigned value for exchange between businesses, people and or both.

The crypto currency actually exists in its own **blockchain**; supported by millions of computers and its own form of crypto software which creates a Bitcoin electronic wallet that can be used to obtain (by standard investment) and then distribute, keep or sell coins or partial coins via encryption from peer to peer (computer to computer).

The decentralized nature of Bitcoin makes it most appealing because no one government agency or financial institution controls or mints, accrues or limits the currency.

A Bitcoin is actually *created* when made. You sit down in front of your computer, and with the current currency you have (i.e. dollars, Pounds, Euros, etc.) invest into and then create a Bitcoin.

You can also buy an existing Bitcoin (or partial coin) from someone else. Bitcoin is not just about transferring money from peer to peer, it also includes some pretty amazing and groundbreaking technology we need to talk about as the monetary aspect is just the tip of the iceberg:

- ✓ Bitcoin is not just a way to pay for something it is a new and exciting Internet technology you can use.

- ✓ Trade is the driving force behind Bitcoin, and so was trust. Bitcoin makes all transactions 100% public so as to no longer need a middleman, credit bureaus, etc.

- ✓ Bitcoin enables all users to keep 100% current and up to date bookkeeping so they know who to trust and what transactions are always valid.

✓ Bitcoin provides all data via one digital and public ledger. There is no need for any other "trusted third party" to facilitate trades, purchases or sales.

✓ This digital ledger is the blockchain that empowers Bitcoin beyond simple transactions; it creates smart and programmable and even exchangeable nodes.

✓ The digital ledger is automatically maintained and updated by "Bitcoin Miners," which is the process of adding transaction records to Bitcoin's public ledger.

✓ Bitcoin mining prevents others from defrauding the system and is also a way to create your own coins inside the blockchain you are working on.

✓ Bitcoin Mining allows for a more stable and decentralized cryptocurrency, thus mining is integral to keeping Bitcoin safe and secure.

There are also some pretty impressive aspects to Bitcoin, as it is far beyond traditional paper money.

Bitcoins are fully "programmable" and have been called smart money as you will soon see.

Smart Money?

Bitcoin may very well be one of the best forms of exchange because the coins can be programmed based on the business or person's needs.

Bitcoin miners use complicated mathematical formulas to both verify and maintain all ledgers. Since every node in the blockchain must agree in order for all ledgers to be congruent, this is huge fraud prevention and a quality assurance consideration that makes everything work well.

Bitcoin miners are rewarded with coins in exchange for this valuable service based on the amount of work they do.

Since all people are encouraged to also become Bitcoin miners, for each additional person that contributes to Bitcoin mining, further speeds the entire process and keeps the system running smoothly, quickly and efficiently.

Any attempt to defraud the system prevents all the nodes from agreeing and thereby rejects any attempts to penetrate the system. This keeps every transaction as public and all nodes must agree or a transaction will not be allowed and this excludes false trades.

This is been referred to as **a shared single source of truth**. In addition, users determine the actual value of their coins based on what they need and the currency melds itself to your needs and can even help you get exactly what you are looking for in trade if you want goods in exchange.

The Value Of A Coin?

The Bitcoin is fully divisible by up to 100,000 units, and each unit is also fully programmable as to when and how it can be used. You can actually **assign properties** to each unit and shape the Bitcoin to do whatever job you need it to accomplish. Try that with a dollar, pound or euro . . .

For example a Bitcoin share could be programmed to represent an exchange of cash, or it could equal a purchase of goods, a share in a co-op, a portion of a crop, a set of tires, or a payment to an electric company.

A Bitcoin can represent **many kinds of property** and it has endless uses for almost any form of exchange.

One way to determine the standard value of the coin is to get an idea of what they are being sold for in the currency of where you live:

Source: http://www.coindesk.com/price/

Once you are aware of the **current value** of the Bitcoin it is simply a matter of dividing and or programming your own portion of the coin as either an instrument of trade, an exchange for money or a way to invest in the future.

For example, you wanted to buy a Bitcoin, you do not need to purchase an entire coin, and you can buy very small parts of a Bitcoin:

Clever marketers have discovered that there are ways to make considerable money off of a Bitcoin even if they just sell small fractions of a coin, as most people want to own even a small amount of this marvelous cryptocurrency.

What About International Trade?

Since Bitcoin is decentralized, that means you can trade with just about anyone worldwide! There are no tariffs, no trade agreements that need to be kept, no chance of being ripped off from someone in a foreign country, the Bitcoin wallet is part of the encrypted technology and the triad of checks and balances that prevent you from being cheated. You are also protected from government intrusion.

There are many wonderful opportunities that exist outside of your current country and being able to exchange value back and forth makes real trade finally possible.

For example, you know it is not possible to send $20,000 in money overseas due to banking restrictions / regulations that prevent the moving and transfer of large amounts of money. Yet a clever person could purchase approximately 30 Bitcoins (at current pricing) and can instantly move this amount of money across borders with NOBODY knowing.

Best of all there are NO fees, NO nosy bureaucrats, NO inept bankers or agencies to deal with. This means that you can now safely and privately use Bitcoin to transfer wealth to just about anyone, anyplace and almost anywhere as long as there is an Internet connection and a computer. This money is 100% secure.

Banks, government agencies and cash controllers truly hate Bitcoin because **it finally puts all of the financial power back into your hands** and the bureaucrats will just have to bother someone else. There is no question that as large international corporations, financial institutions and even governments attempts to manipulate and control currencies, Bitcoin is the future.

As economies continue to collapse, Bitcoin continues to gain value as millions begin to see the potential.

How To Invest Safely In Bitcoin

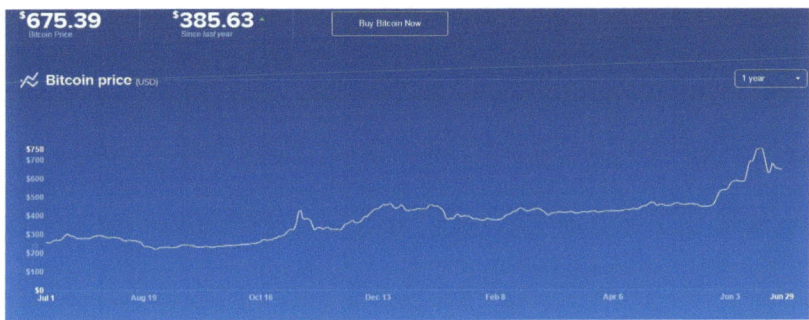

Source: https://www.coinbase.com/charts

Bitcoin was not considered a serious investment until 2013. Now everybody is talking about the investment potential for not only their own investments, but as a serious form of trade that has the potential to be used worldwide.

In fact, people are beginning to catch on and are investing! So how should the average person consider investing? One financial investor discusses this:

"The simplest way the Average Joe can invest in Bitcoin is to outright buy some. Buying BTC today is simpler than ever, with many established firms in the US and abroad involved in the business of buying and selling bitcoins. For investors in the USA, the simplest solution is Coinbase. The company sells BTC to customers at a mark-up that is usually around 1% over the current market price."

Source: http://www.investopedia.com/articles/investing/082914/basics-buying-and-investing-bitcoin.asp

For most people, especially for Americans, **Coinbase.com** is useful when it comes to Bitcoin investment. You can also automate your purchasing via linking your bank account directly to your coinbase wallet.

This is useful if you simply want to "float" a certain amount of money into your Bitcoin investing. For example, if you want to invest $200 each month in partial Bitcoins, so simply set up the auto buy feature.

While this may seem to take away from not having a third party verification system in place, understand that this is one of the easiest ways to begin investing, and all of your money can be put back into Bitcoin investments you feel are worthwhile.

Like anything there will always be caveats when dealing with a third-party. Even though Coinbase is a reputable way to get Bitcoins, understand that you are buying your coin directly from the company and not another Bitcoin owner.

The company devotes a considerable amount of time to sourcing good purchases of Bitcoins. This can create issues as far as the ways it comes to securing holdings during ongoing volatility of the market.

Have a look at the link and decide if this is the right option for you: https://www.coinbase.com/

Other Ways To Invest

Once you've acquired a few coins, you may want to consider a traditional Bitcoin exchange.

The advantage is that you are removing the middleman but as with all exchanges there is a small fee that is to be paid, between .02% and .05% depending on how many trades you have done recently.

Another way you could consider buying, selling and/or trading Bitcoins is to use a special website that matches buyers and sellers worldwide:

"I found Weston on Local Bitcoins, a Finnish company that connects Bitcoin buyers and sellers around the globe. With buyers in 190 countries and 3,317 cities, it's the widest reaching peer-to-peer Bitcoin exchange. There are 100+ active sellers in Washington, DC alone. Richard had a "reputation score" of a perfect 100, which certainly endeared me to him."

Source: http://readwrite.com/2013/10/23/i-bought-bitcoin-in-person-and-heres-what-happened/

The commentary above is just one of the thousands of satisfied customers that use the website:

https://localbitcoins.com/

The site brings buyers and sellers together in the nearest possible location if they choose to meet. You can conduct an entire sale or purchase without having to meet face to face either, but there are times meeting speeds the process.

Adding Bitcoin To Your Business

According to Coinbase, more than 25,000 merchants are using Bitcoin as a payment option and a payment processor, just with their platform. Others, like BitPay, claim they have over 20,000 registered as well.

This is a huge change from just a few years ago, when just a few hundred individuals were utilizing and exchanging Bitcoins for products and services:

"According to Coinbase, on 27th of February 2014, the company has hit one million Coinbase consumer wallets. At the start of 2013 that figure was under 13,000. That is an astounding growth rate of 7,592.31%. As more people start using the upcoming virtual currency, more merchants are bound to follow suit and adopt it into their payment systems."

Source: http://fitsmallbusiness.com/how-to-accept-bitcoin-payments/

Clearly, Bitcoin's are here to stay. Not only is this a way to accrue Bitcoins, but there are some rather impressive reasons why any business should consider taking Bitcoin payments:

- ✓ **Lower fees** – the typical credit card processing fee takes about 3% cut of every credit card transaction. During the course of the year this can add up to thousands of dollars.

- ✓ **No Chargebacks** - one of the most annoying things about being in business are when people simply forget that they made purchase and claim a chargeback or are attempting to defraud you. Bitcoin transactions are irreversible.

- ✓ **No Fraud Possible** - again, because Bitcoin payments are not reversible, this almost completely eliminates other forms of payment fraud that have become so prevalent utilizing larger financial institutions.

✓ **New Way To Pay** - one thing we have all learned in business is the more ways to offer clients or customers pay, the happier they are. People want to use cryptocurrencies as they know the benefits.

Adding Bitcoin as one of your payment options is actually fairly simple. This is because there are several major payment processor companies, like Coinbase that have streamlined the process.

For example, if you have worked with PayPal, then you are aware of how you can simply access their business tools, create payment buttons and then embed them on your website.

Coinbase not only allows for the buying, selling and transfer of Bitcoins, but they also have a very easy way (cut and paste) to use specific merchant tools that practically automate the entire process.

Have a look here and see for yourself how easy it is:

https://developers.coinbase.com/docs/merchants/payment-buttons

Pretty simple. As business owners we are in a unique position to benefit by accepting crypto currencies.

Not only is this a great way to build up some potential savings, but the more that you use Bitcoin, the easier it will become to understand its benefits as well as how you can use Bitcoin to further grow your own business.

What Is Ethereum?

Ethereum is a public blockchain platform with programmable transaction functionality. It provides a decentralized virtual machine that can execute peer-to-peer contracts using a cryptocurrency called ether.

Ethereum - Wikipedia, the free encyclopedia
https://en.wikipedia.org/wiki/**Ethereum**   Wikipedia ▾

Source: https://en.wikipedia.org/wiki/Ethereum

Blockchains are here to stay. They offer unparalleled protection and the ability to create and sustain unstoppable applications that can be utilized or even overlaid with existing technology.

Ethereum is a powerful blockchain platform that can make endless possibilities a reality for people, organizations and business.

In a world of overreaching bureaucracy, fraud, waste, employee collusion and corporate spying, the Ethereum platform offers real solutions for:

✓ Developers looking to protect their intellectual property.

✓ Entrepreneurs who want to invest in these new developmental platforms.

✓ Investors can also benefit by funding projects that have the potential to sweep the Internet.

✓ Platforms that can meld into almost anything people want it to be and they are fully decentralized.

As a blockchain Ethereum offers all the nuts and bolts, bringing these people together allows for new technology to have a powerful and protected incubation period. Once fully explored, developers, entrepreneurs and investors each benefit from the relationship:

"Ethereum is a decentralized platform that runs smart contracts: applications that run exactly as programmed without any possibility of downtime, censorship, fraud or third party interference."

Source: https://www.ethereum.org/

If you are looking for a way to either participate in or create new applications using blockchains, this is a great place to start. The wall materials necessary create a decentralized series of Patients is perhaps one of the most powerful this utilization of the Internet.

Ethereum is a great example of how any industry or individual person can benefit by creating their own blockchain and using it to expand business, personal, social and even political aspirations.

Understand that Ethereum is not a cryptocurrency, but rather a series of tools that hand you the keys to creating and sustaining your very own high-powered blockchain:

"Ethereum is an alternative decentralized ledger protocol, not an alternative cryptocurrency. Ethereum's ideological lineage contains as much BitTorrent, Java and Freenet as it does Bitcoin. From a product perspective, it is a general-purpose, global blockchain that can govern both financial and non-financial types of application states."

Source: https://blog.ethereum.org/2015/05/24/the-business-imperative-behind-the-ethereum-vision/

Technologies like Ethereum are beginning to expand across the Internet. This bodes well for the ongoing and continuous use of blockchains to:

- ✓ Protect people's intellectual property
- ✓ Keep anyone from ever interfering in your business
- ✓ Limit personal data leaks and hacking
- ✓ Protect the project, even if people leave
- ✓ Keep the government out of your business

There are certainly many other advantages to using a wonderful platform like Ethereum.

The sky is the limit. With open source materials that can be utilized, now it is possible to build and distribute decentralized applications.

This means without middlemen to help you accomplish this. Everything is based on single transactions directly between people, without third parties and is censorship free.

Conclusion

The point of discussing Ethereum was to demonstrate how technology **is offering real solutions** to people who need it. Platforms like Ethereum are beginning to appear all across the Internet as they offer what we all need to thrive.

As society, financial institutions, governments all rely on third party trust verification, isn't it nice to know that new and emerging technologies via blockchains are beginning to appear across a wide spectrum of business, personal and social technologies.

Ethereum is just one of the most recent and successful versions of what people are now demanding; privacy, protection from financial loss, a reduction or even elimination of dealing with bureaucracies and a way for people to come together and exchange value back and forth.

Everything the elites HATE for us little people; power, freedom and choice.

As long as there is money to be made, governments, crooked politicians, hackers, and criminals are just some of the obstacles and challenges that must be met in order to provide a safe and secure future.

We see the world as it is now – too centralized.

You should take time to strongly consider involving yourself in investing at least **some of your savings** into cryptocurrencies like Bitcoin.

The future looks extremely interesting because the utilization of cryptocurrencies can allow people to create and sustain the exact kind of income and/or trade necessary for their own personal and business growth.

For example, if you are an artist and you decide to sell some of your intellectual property, you could create your own cryptocurrency. This allows people to invest in YOU, with no tendrils from your bank or government.

You can actually create currency that is assigned specifically to you and your business. That currency can then be openly traded on certain platforms and can come to have its own intrinsic value over time to patrons and even strangers.

It is possible for there to be MILLIONS of unique and highly specific types of crypto currencies in circulation. At this time there certainly are as people are discovering smart money is a wonderful solution.

Because this currency is decentralized, you are creating a form of token economy that has the ability to grow well beyond its simplistic origins. Such currency can be exchanged for real or trade values, centralized currencies like the dollar or the euro; whatever value you wish to assign to the currency works. This is impossible in our current centralized, third-party trust, fraudulent banking model, because the value of currency is simply its cash value, and nothing else. Yet your OWN currencies can take on a life of their own.

For example, let's say you wanted to start a babysitting business. The owner would issue their own form of currency and require people to make payments directly through the cryptocurrency link on her website.

You might wonder why someone would do this. Here are some great reasons why this is a fabulous idea:

- ✓ **You get paid regardless** - because you are asking to be paid by your own currency, refunds or any attempt to get money that you have been paid back is NOT possible. All transactions with digital money are final.

- ✓ **The valuation of your own currency increases** - by utilizing your own currency and creating and sustaining a valuable commodity that over time can be exchanged and used by other people, the same way that Bitcoin's can be utilized.

✓ **Encourage others to use cryptocurrency** - the more people you involve and educate with cryptocurrencies, the larger your currency will circulate and thereby have the potential to be used in other exchanges.

✓ **Be your own bank** - becoming your own bank means that you never have to worry about insufficient funds, bounced checks, chargebacks or any other of the nasty financial games banks play and you pay.

All of these reasons are just the tip of the iceberg. Taking back your own financial power and privacy cannot be overstated in a world where all of this information is so routinely to less than honest business entities.

In this EBook we have discussed everything you need to know about cryptocurrencies, and how the current trust based system is seriously flawed as it allows singular points of attack. This means your money is never really safe. Since we all want money, we have had to rely on these institutions to keep our money safe.

Yet we have seen it is not and that the latest emerging technologies are attempting to compensate.

Blockchains offer real solutions. Bitcoin is an excellent example of how this technology can offer us a chance to break free from debt enslavement; finally we can create smart money that will serve us and our needs, not just line the pockets of middlemen.

If you found this book helpful, please share a couple of sentences and a 4-5 star review on Amazon. It would mean a great deal to me and others who are considering purchasing this book.

If you have any questions or comments, feel free to email me at rj@notraceleft.com I try to reply to all questions that come in and that I am able to.

Thank you for reading **Blockchain Explained: Technology Guide to the Bitcoin and Cryptocurrency Fintech Revolution**

Best of luck, and be informed!

R.J. Simmons

P.S. This book couldn't cover everything, but we know you now have enough information to make some informed choices with the future of your money.

Our wealth and privacy is constantly under attack and for all of my readers, I give you complimentary updates to the latest threats to your personal and financial information – with solutions and steps to take to protect yourself.

STAY connected by Subscribing to our FREE Newsletter:

www.NoTraceLeft.com

Additional Resources

https://www.bitcoin.com/

https://bitcoin.org/en/

http://weusecoins.com/

http://www.coinbase.com

https://www.reddit.com/r/Bitcoin

https://www.quora.com/topic/Bitcoin

http://www.investopedia.com/terms/b/bitcoin.asp

https://www.blockchain.com/

http://www.notraceleft.com/

I

www.ingramcontent.com/pod-product-compliance
Lightning Source LLC
Chambersburg PA
CBHW040922180526
45159CB00002BA/572